How to Make Origami Airplanes That Fly

GERY HSU

DOVER PUBLICATIONS, INC.
New York

For my brother David

Published in Canada by General Publishing Company, Ltd., 30 Lesmill Road, Don Mills, Toronto, Ontario.

How to Make Origami Airplanes That Fly is a new work, first published by Dover Publications, Inc., in 1992.

Manufactured in the United States of America
Dover Publications, Inc., 31 East 2nd Street, Mineola, N.Y. 11501

Library of Congress Cataloging-in-Publication Data

Hsu, Gery.
    How to make origami airplanes that fly / Gery Hsu.
        p.   cm.
    ISBN 0-486-27352-0 (pbk.)
    1. Paper airplanes. 2. Origami. I. Title.
TL778.H78 1992
745.592—dc20
                                                                        92-21692
                                                                        CIP

TABLE OF CONTENTS

INTRODUCTION

PURE ORIGAMI is an ancient and elegant art; making paper airplanes is a pastime of relatively recent origin. Origami is concerned with beauty whereas paper-airplane folders usually place a premium on performance. In addition, origamians tend to follow strict conventions while paper-airplane folders may create their own rules as long as they have fun. Combining the two paperfolding activities creates a conflict of requirements, with one side encouraging more detail and the other demanding more paper allocation to the wings. This collection is dedicated to people who are origamians, paper-airplane fanatics, or both, or neither for that matter, as everyone can find interest in the challenge to excel in both art and air. All of the planes can fly, and each is made from a single unaltered square sheet of paper.

Each of the twelve models within represents a different balance between detail, function and difficulty. The first set of instructions is for the Jet Tail, a component of many of the more difficult models diagrammed later. In general, the models become more challenging as the book progresses, so an efficient approach would begin with the first model, the Space Shuttle, and go on from there. Each fold must be made extremely accurately, especially in the more advanced models. A hastily folded model may appear to be correctly folded but probably will not fly as well as one that is well made. Patience during the construction of the origami plane will prevent frustration when it comes to flying it.

When following the diagrams, the folder should have a mental picture of the entire folding sequence for the model as well as a good idea of how the completed model is to appear. It is a good idea to look over all diagrams before doing any folding. Also, look closely at the photographs for additional information. The photographs become especially useful when completing the model, since many of the small details are not illustrated in the instructions. These details will naturally vary from one paperfolder to another depending on personal artistic expression.

5⅞" kami-weight origami paper is appropriate since the resulting models tend to have the proper rigidity and strength. Larger paper tends to produce flimsy planes and smaller paper is difficult to work with. Thin typing paper cut into a square is also adequate, though the rough edge created when making the square can foil precise folding.

I hope you will have as much fun with my air force as I had in creating it. Good luck—and happy flying!

SYMBOLS

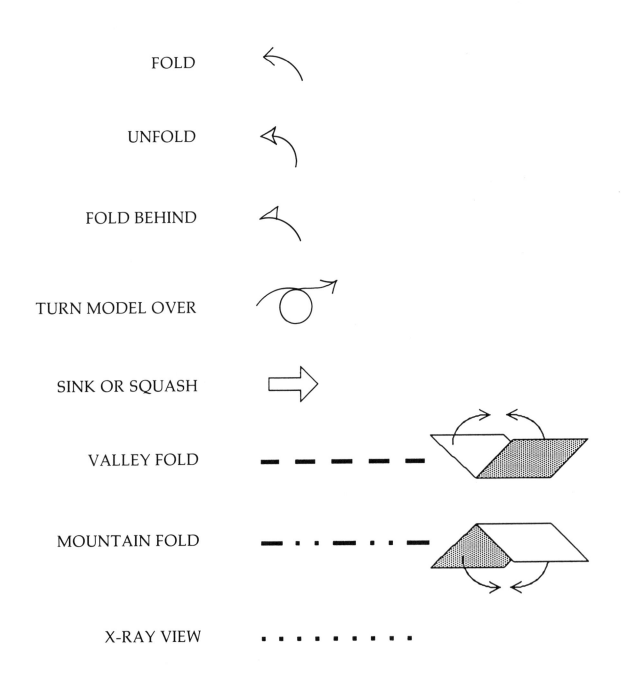

FOLD

UNFOLD

FOLD BEHIND

TURN MODEL OVER

SINK OR SQUASH

VALLEY FOLD

MOUNTAIN FOLD

X-RAY VIEW

JET TAIL

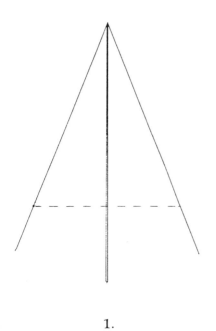

1.

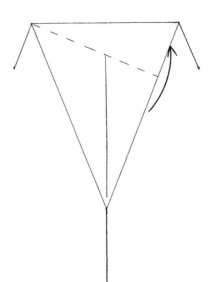

2. Align the edge indicated with itself.

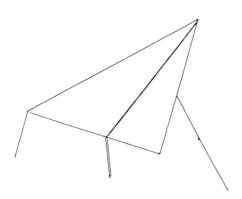

3. Result of step 2. Undo.
    Repeat for other side.

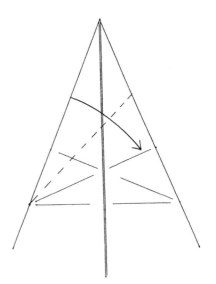

4. Align edge with crease made in step 2.

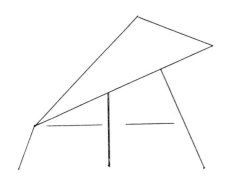

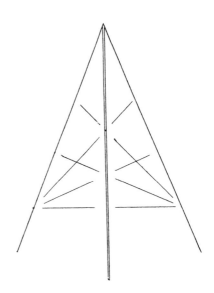

5.   Result of step 4. Undo.
     Repeat for other side.

6.   Completely unfold.

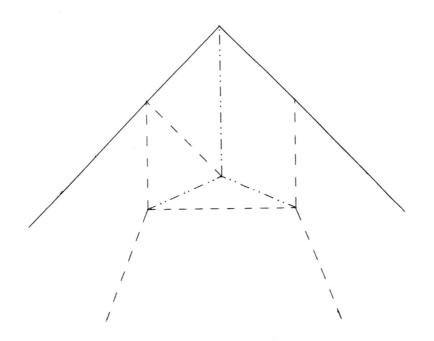

7.   Make folds as shown.

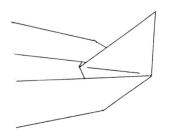

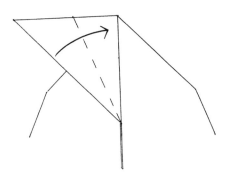

8. Slightly opened view of step 7.

9. Align the edge with the midline. The crease formed marks the location of the fold on the subjacent layer shown in step 10.

Type A

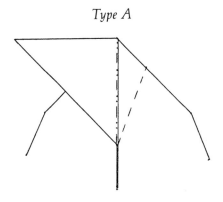

10*A*. Repeat for other side.

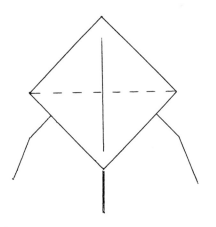

11*A*.

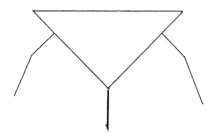

12*A*. Type *A* JET TAIL complete.

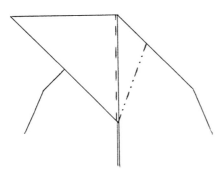

10*B*. Turn over.

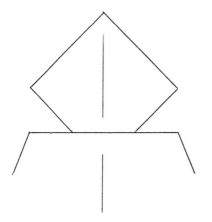

11*B*.

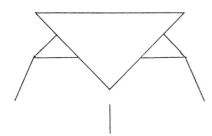

12*B*. Type *B* JET TAIL complete.

SPACE SHUTTLE

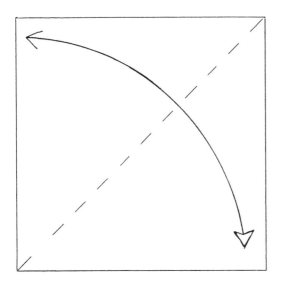

1.

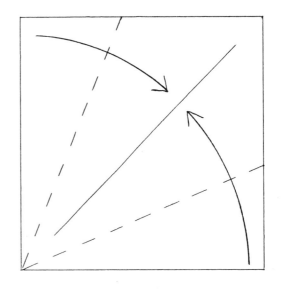

2.

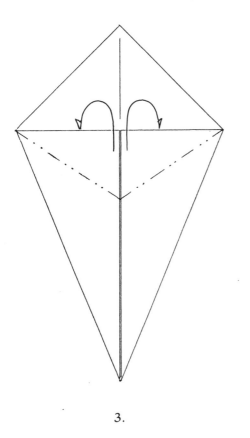

3.

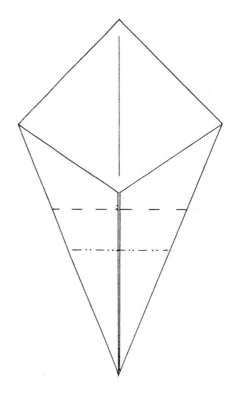

4. Approximate these folds.

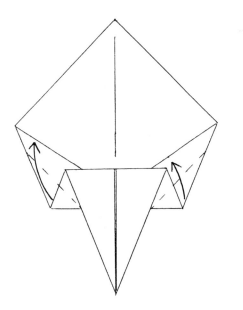 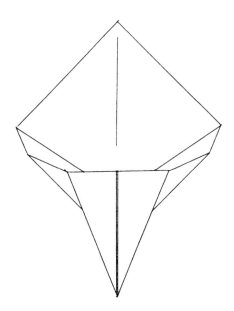

5. Look at step 6 to see where this fold goes.

6. Turn over.

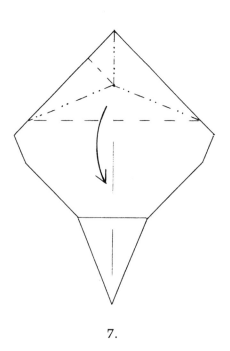

7.

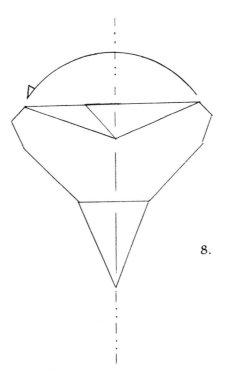

8.

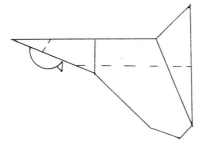

9. Tuck front under and fold wings out.

FUTURISTIC SHUTTLE

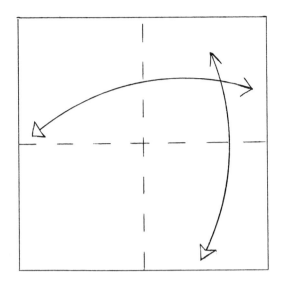

1.

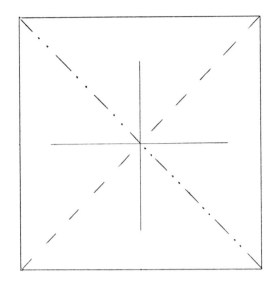

2. Fold along with creases made in step 1.

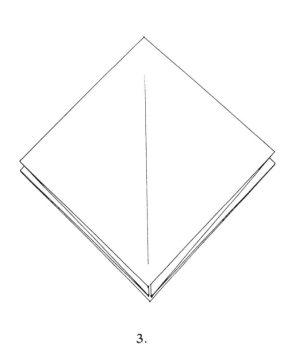

3.

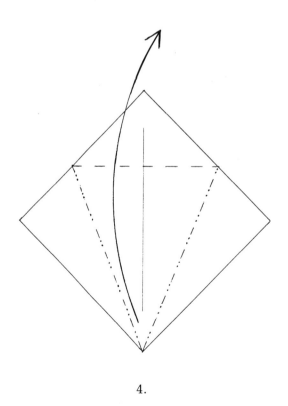

4.

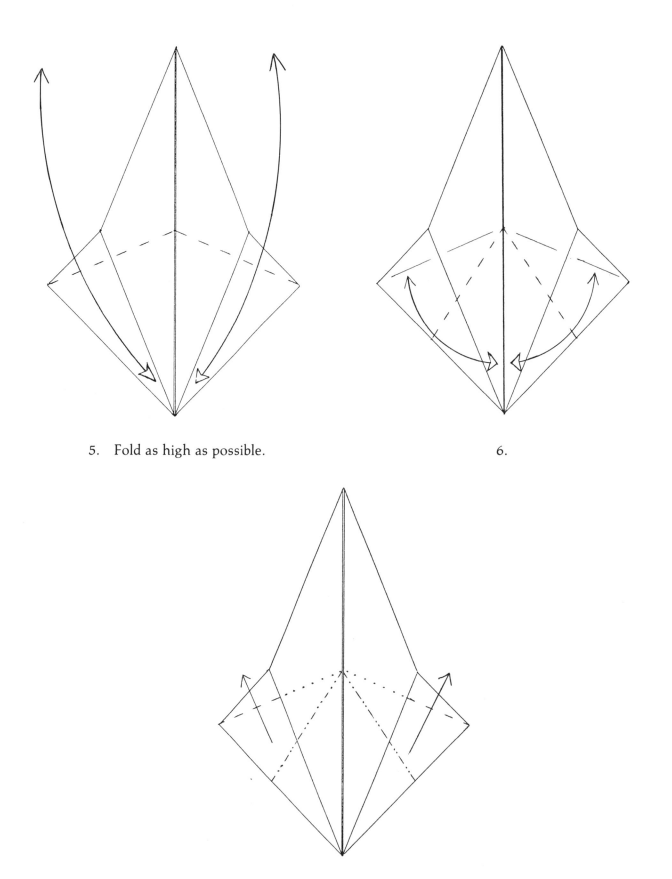

5. Fold as high as possible.

6.

7. Note how the mountain fold seems to traverse two layers. Actually, the layers separate to make two mountain folds. Also, the valley fold does not affect the top layer.

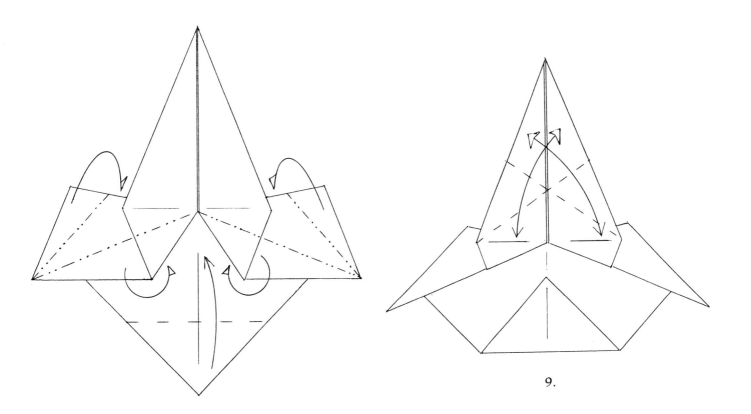

8.   Result of step 7.

9.

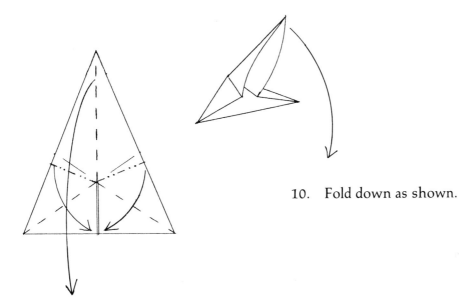

10.   Fold down as shown.

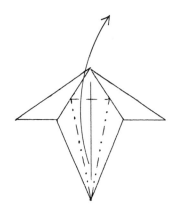

11.

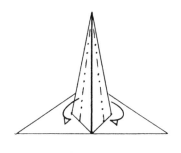

12.

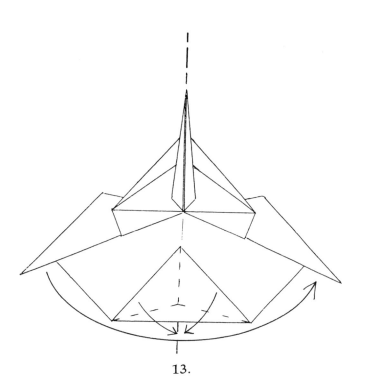

13.

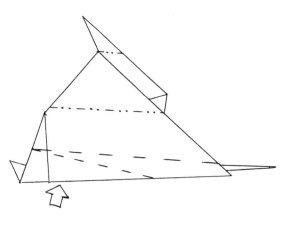

14.   Push tail up and form wings.

FLYING WING

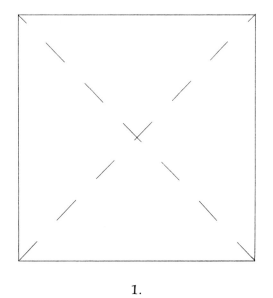

1.

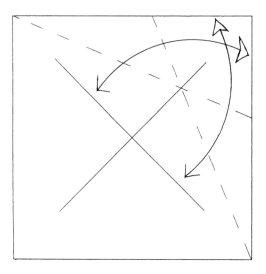

2.

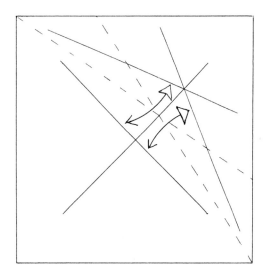

3.

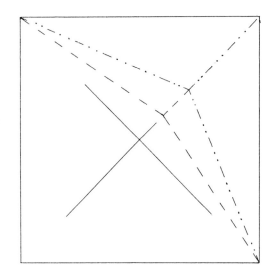

4. Flatten tail to one side. See step 5.

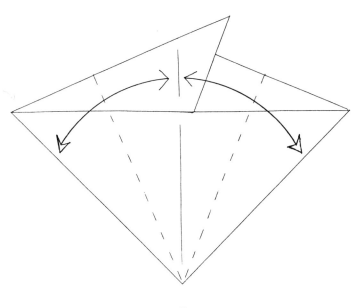

5.

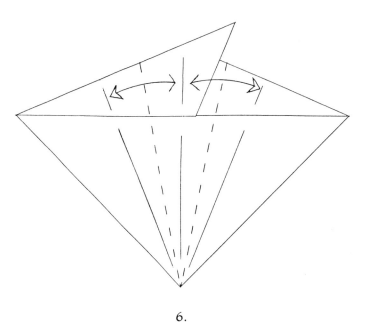

6.

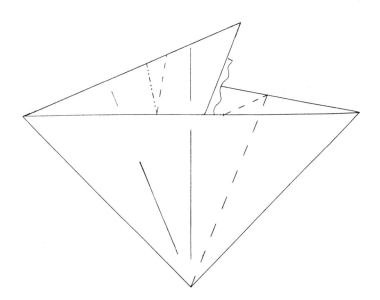

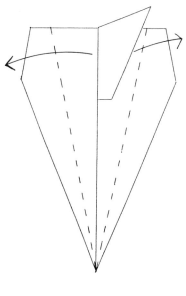

8.

7. The top layer is cut away on the right side for clarity. The folds shown on the left should also be made on the right side concurrently with the folds shown on the right. Look at step 9 for clarification.

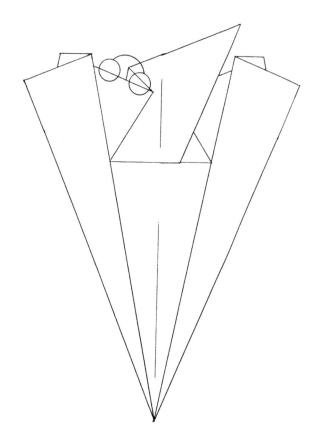

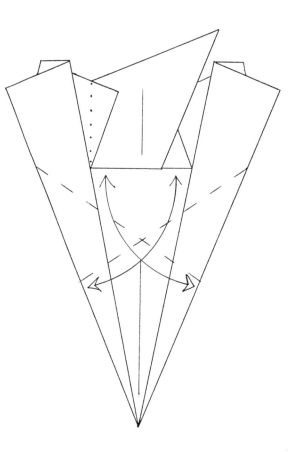

9. Align the edge with itself (match the circled areas).

10.

11. Flatten tip to one side.

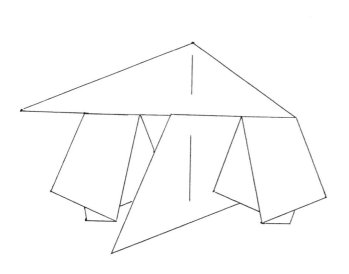

12. Flatten tip centrally.

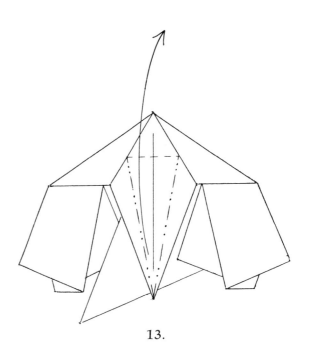

13.

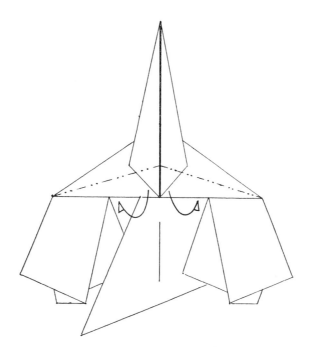

14. Tuck under.

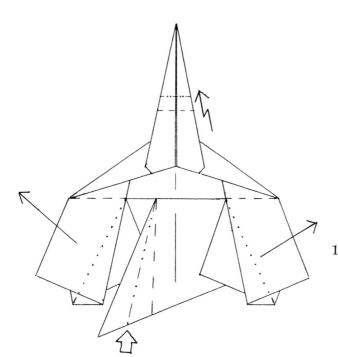

15. Refer to the photograph for clarification.

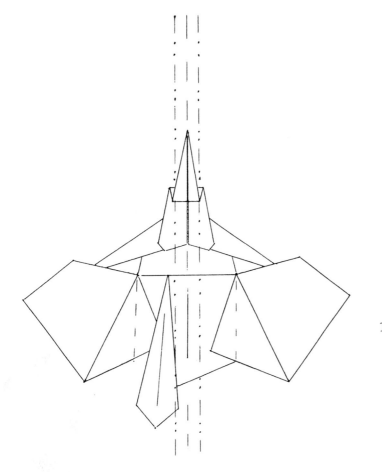

16. Round the engines and refer to the photograph for details.

INTERCEPTOR

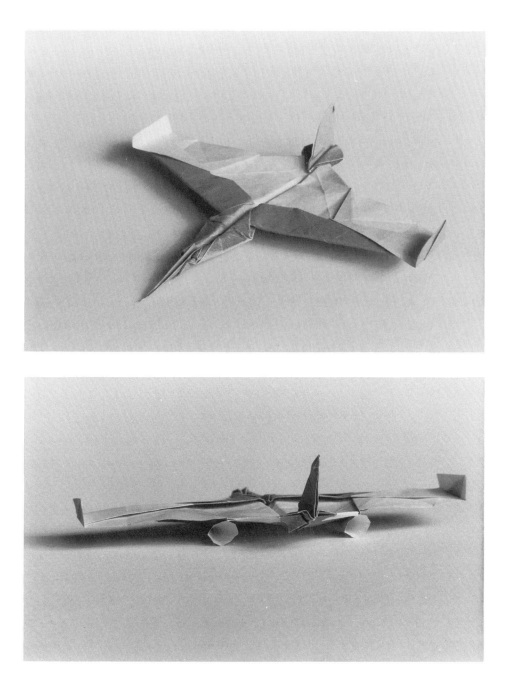

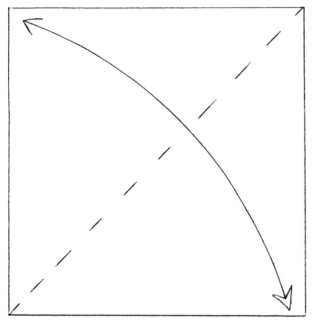

1.

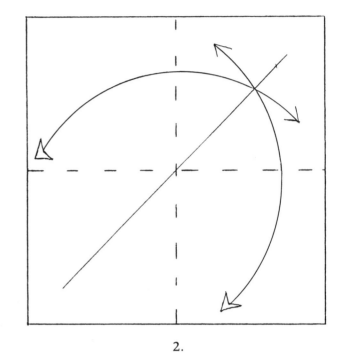

2.

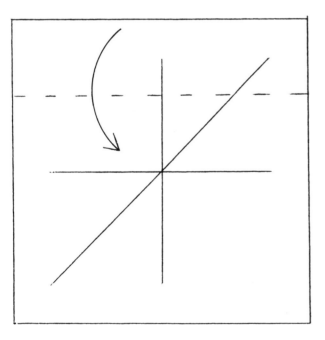

3.

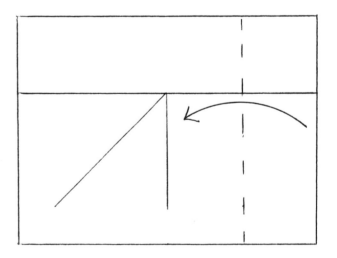

4.

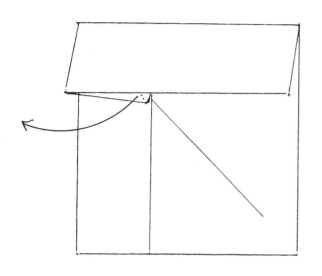

5.

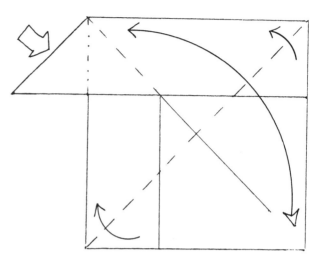

6.

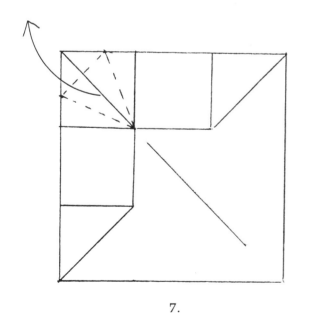

7.

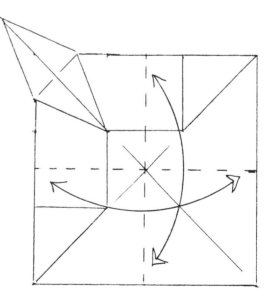

8.

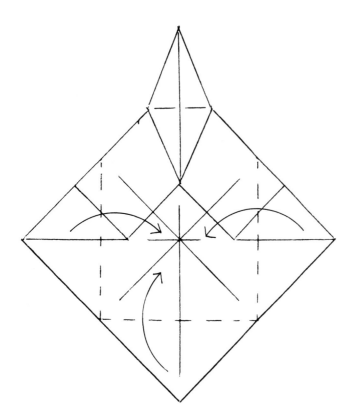

9. Turn over when done.

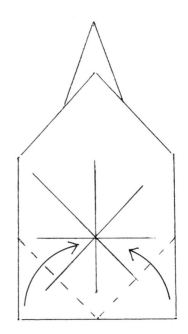

10. Turn over again.

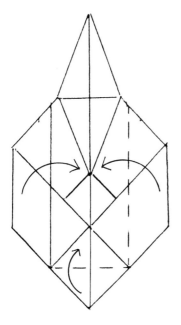

11. Turn over again.

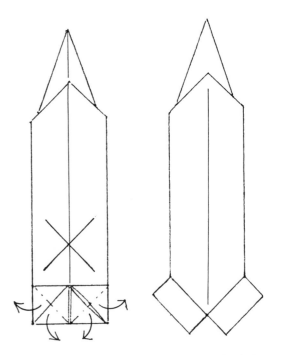

12. Spread out as shown on the left to get the structure on the right. Completely unfold when done.

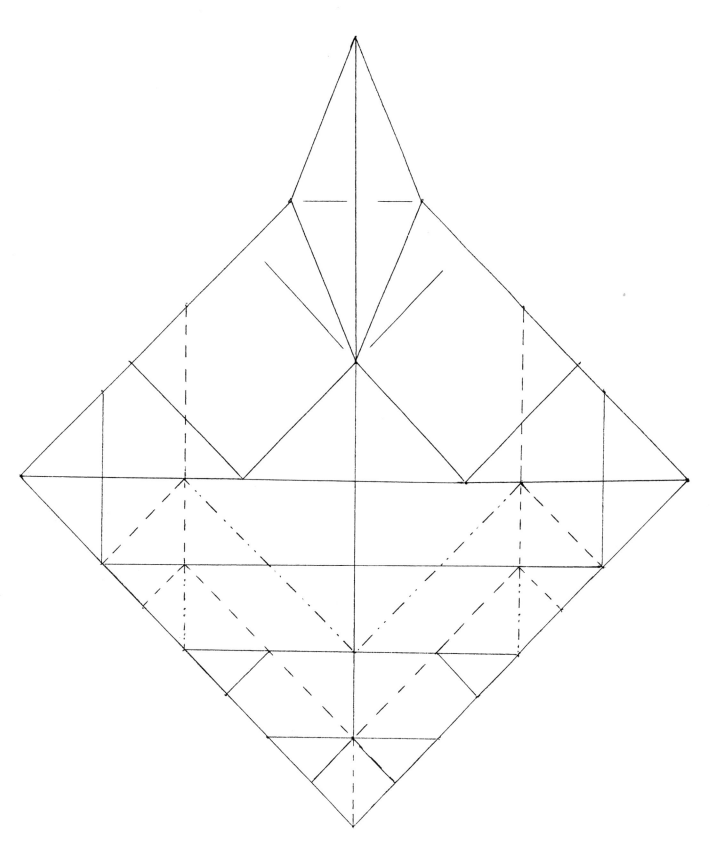

13.

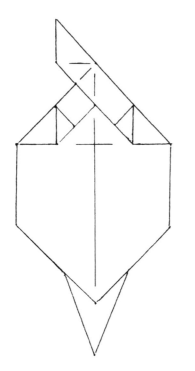

14.　View of underside of plane.

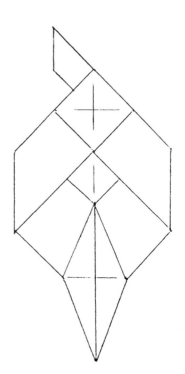

15.　View of top.

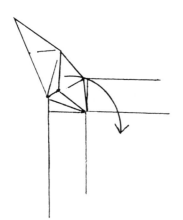

16.　Underside. Flatten.

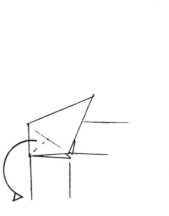
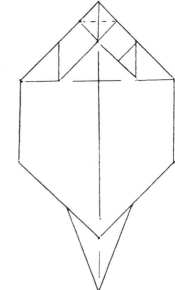

17.　Fold tail to top side of plane. The location of the fold is shown in both diagrams.

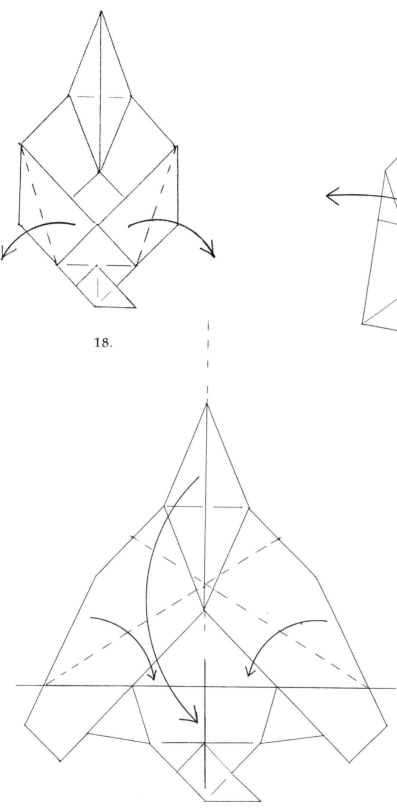

18.

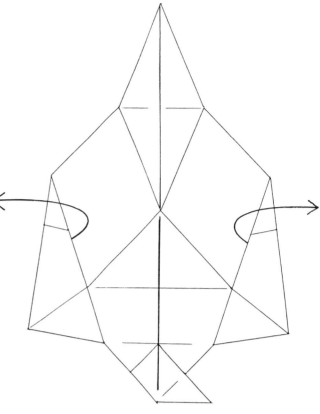

19.   Pull out and flatten.

20.

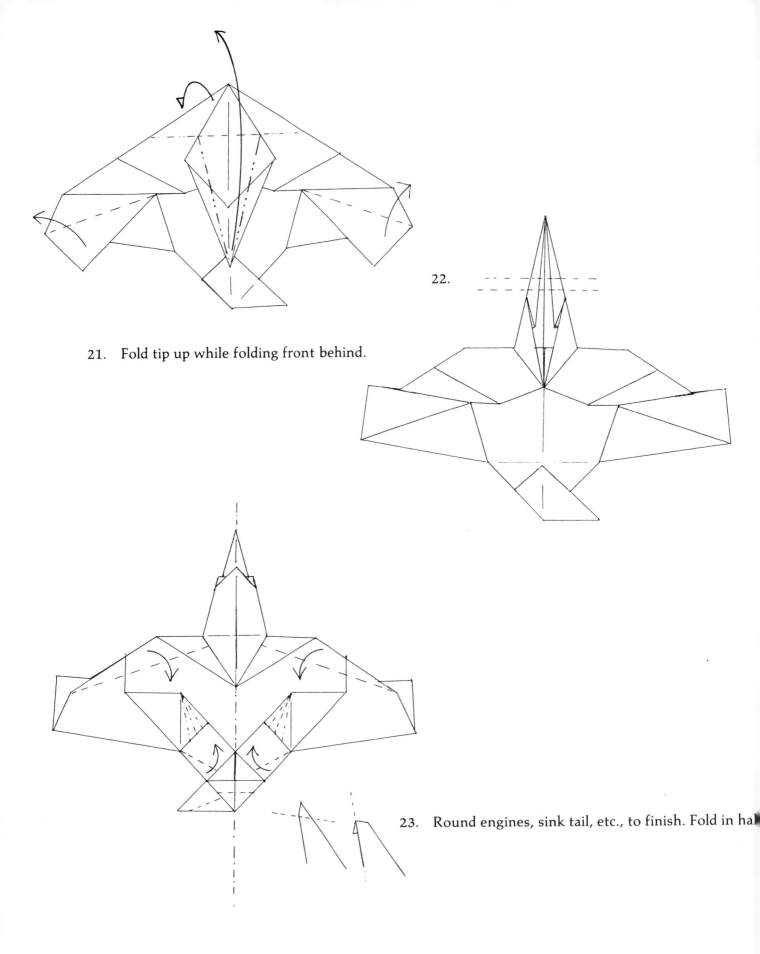

21. Fold tip up while folding front behind.

22.

23. Round engines, sink tail, etc., to finish. Fold in ha[l]

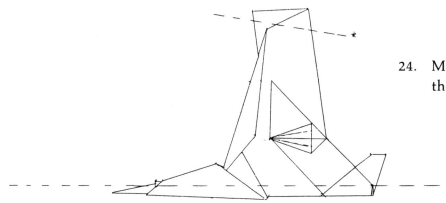

24. Make wings. Stabilizing flaps on the ends of the wings are optional.

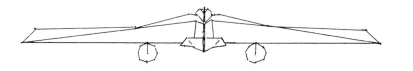

25. Rear view.

26. Form wings into the shapes shown here.

JET I

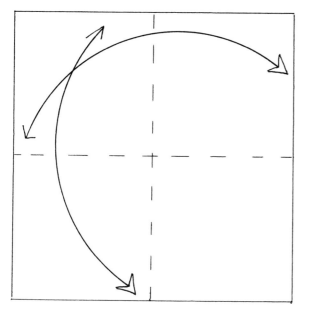

1.

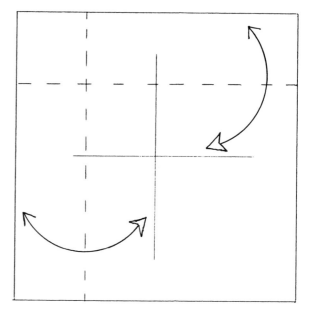

2.

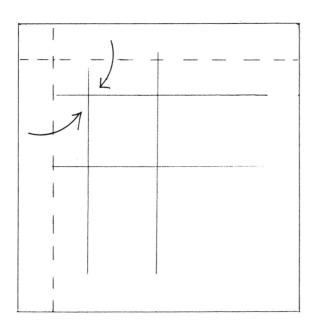

3.

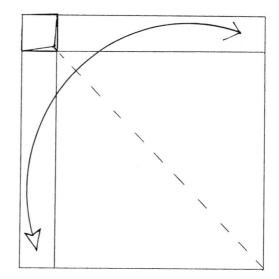

4. Turn model over when done.

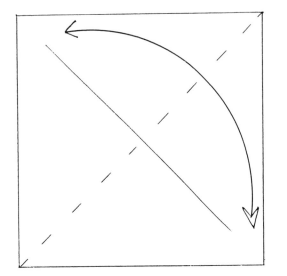

5. Turn back over.

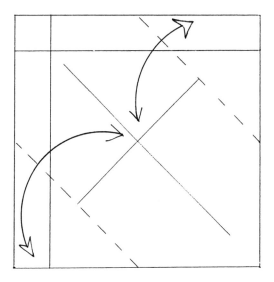

6.

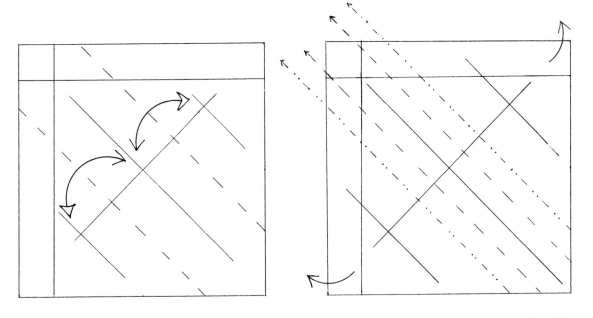

7.

8. Extend folds shown by unfolding flaps.

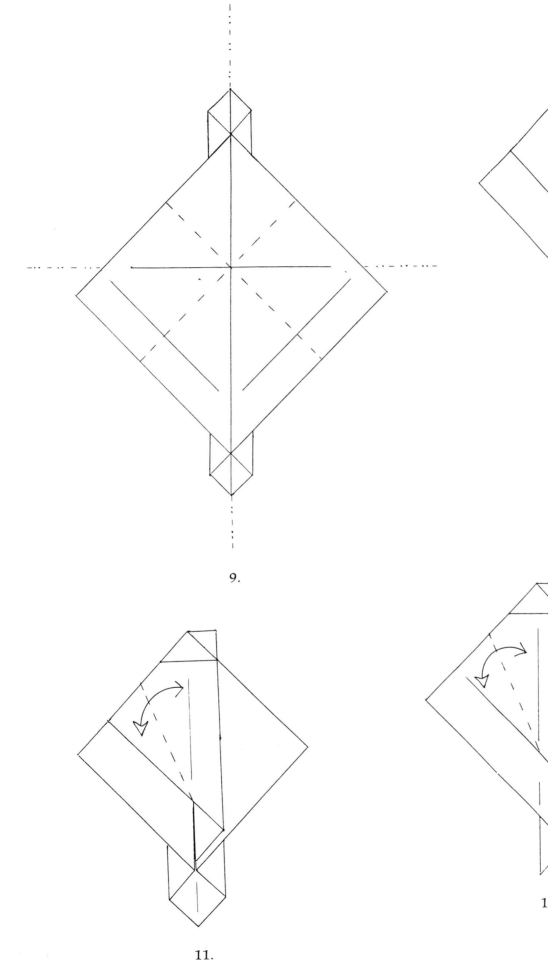

9.

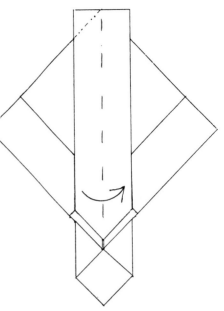

10.

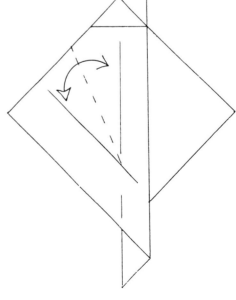

11.

12.

13.

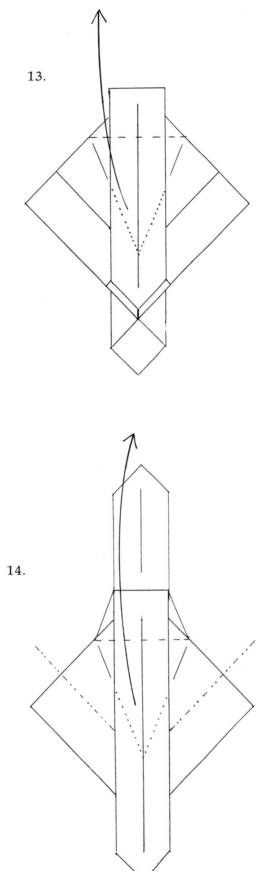

Steps 1 through 14 are essentially making what is commonly called a "Bird Base" *except* with one side having an extended border.

14.

15. Make diverging creases as shown while flattening the tip downward.

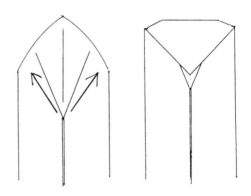

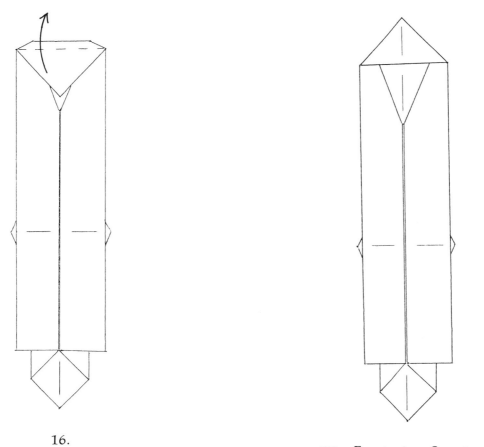

16.

17.   Erect wing. See step 18.

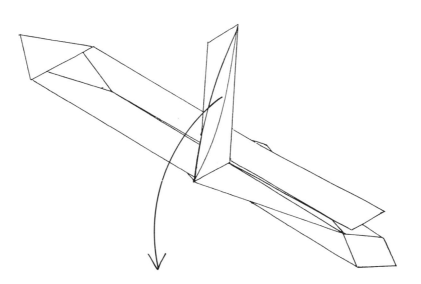

18.   Separate the two triangles and flatten.
See step 20 for the orientation of the wings. Note that the wings
are not flattened perpendicularly to the axis of the plane.

19.   Step 18 in progress.

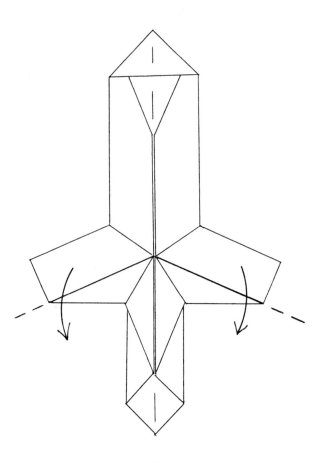

20.

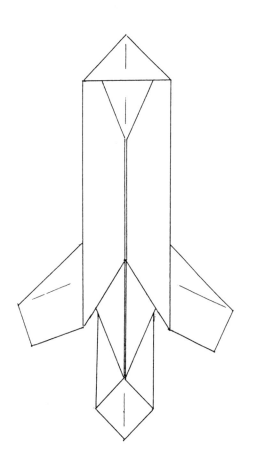

21.   Refold wing under the front of the plane.
      Compare the model in step 19 to the one in 22.

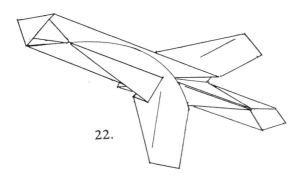

22.

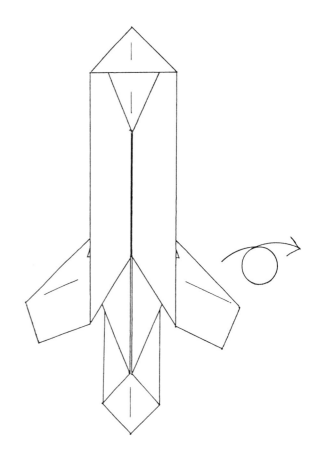

23. Result of reorientation of wing.

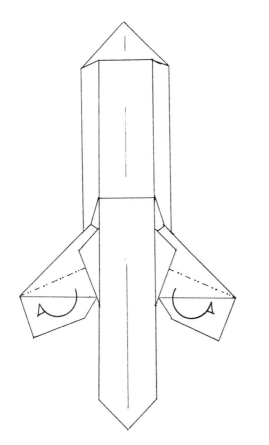

24. Tuck under.

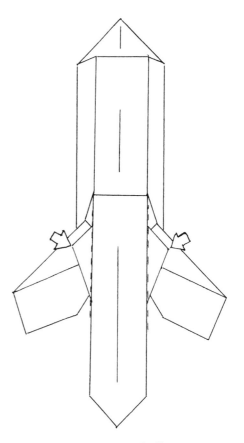

25. Squash flat.

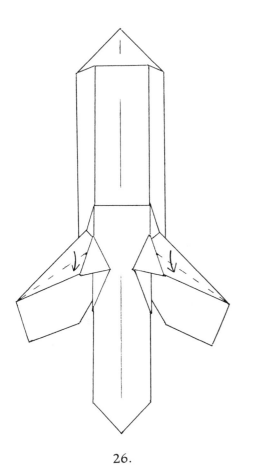

26.

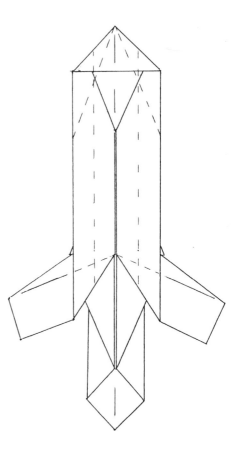

27.   Prepare these creases.

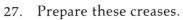

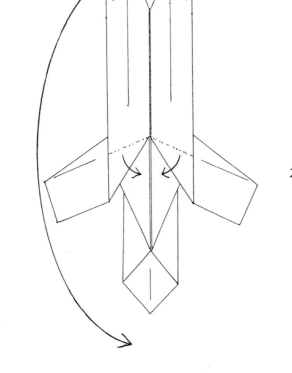

28.   Fold down while noting the mountain folds.

44   Jet I

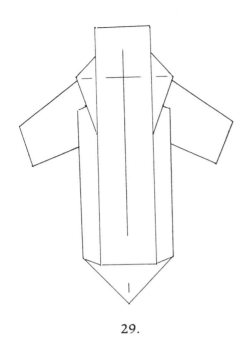

29.

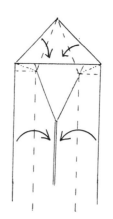

30.   Fold the front up concurrently.

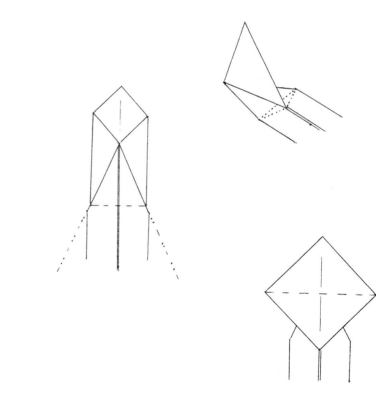

31.

32.   Make mountain folds along the diagonal edges and a valley fold on the bottom layer of the tail and flatten to get the structure in the top right of the diagram. Spread out as with the JET TAIL.

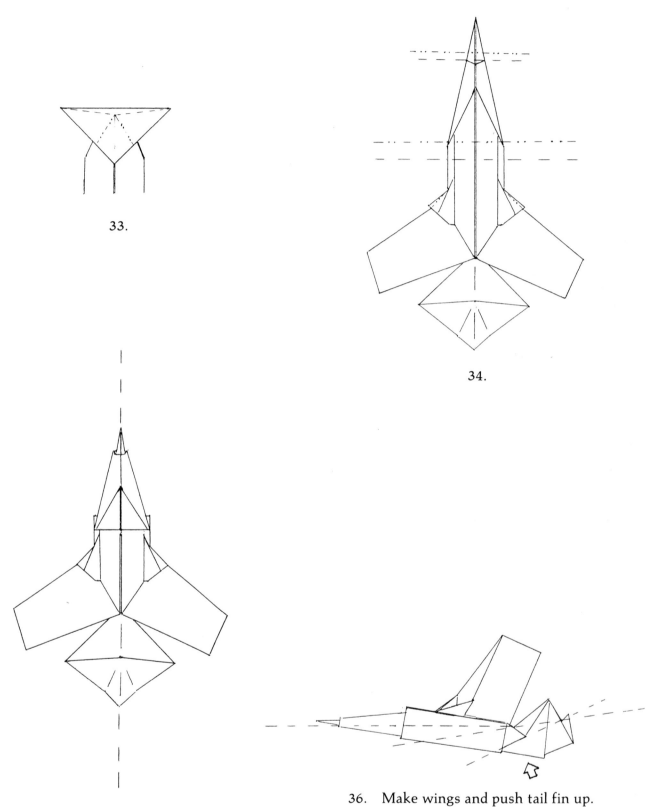

33.

34.

35.

36.   Make wings and push tail fin up.

DELTA WING JET

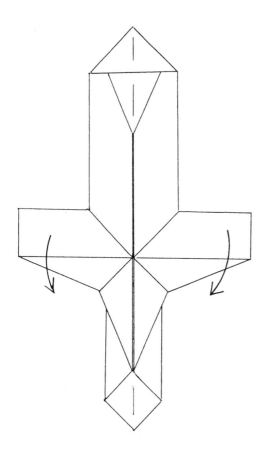

1. Start with step 18 of JET I *except:*
   align wings perpendicular to plane.

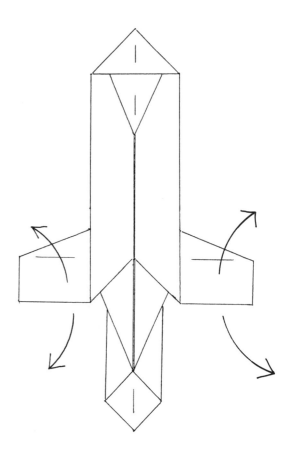

2. Separate layers of wings
   and flatten against plane.

3. Repeat process on other side.

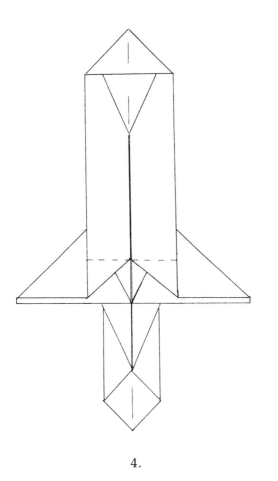

4.

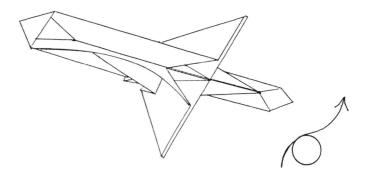

5. Reverse orientation of wing
    as in step 19 of JET I.

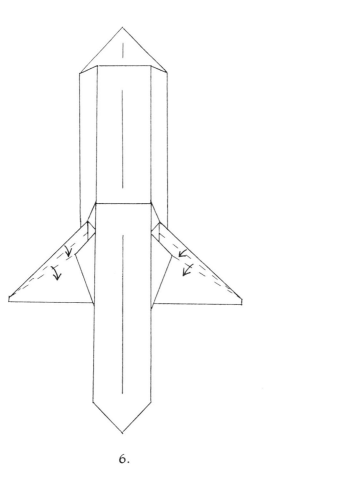

6.

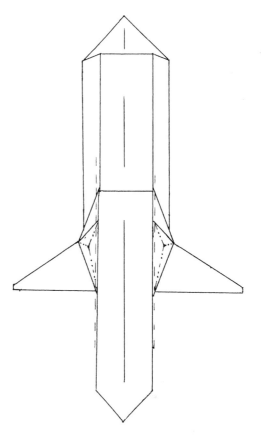

7. Make sides into wheels.

JET II

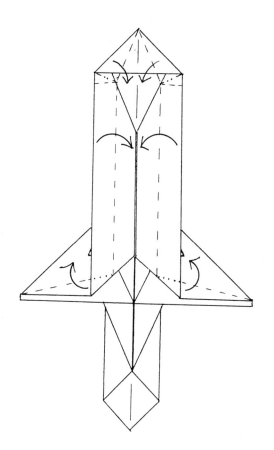

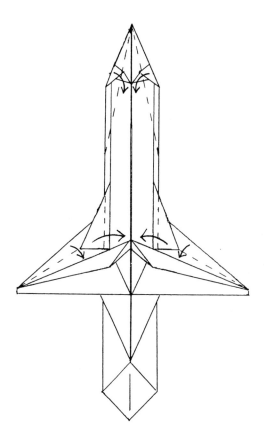

1. Begin with the DELTA WING JET step 5.

2. The triangles in the middle should be made into wheels upon completion of the plane. Also, make Type *B* JET TAIL.

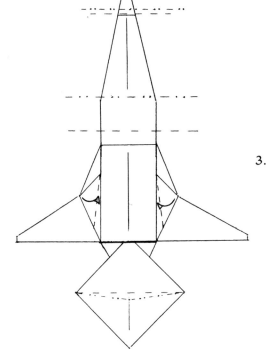

3. Tuck the sides into the body of the plane.

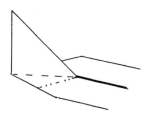

4. Complete.

DOUBLE TAIL FIGHTER

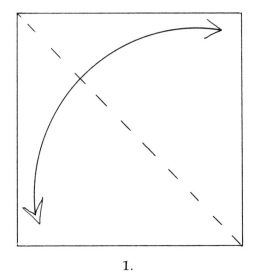

1.

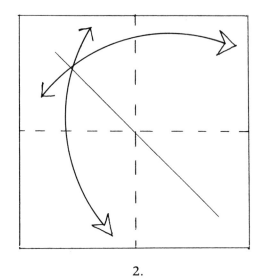

2.

3.

4.

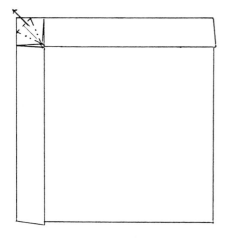

5.

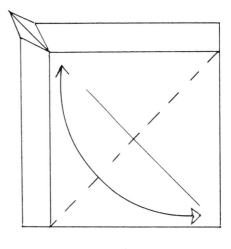

6.

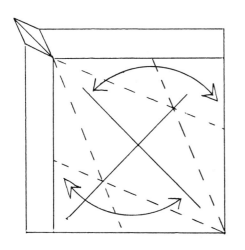

7.

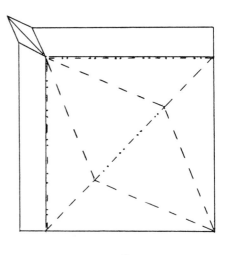

8.

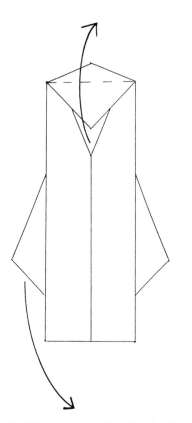

9. Fold tip up and backside down.

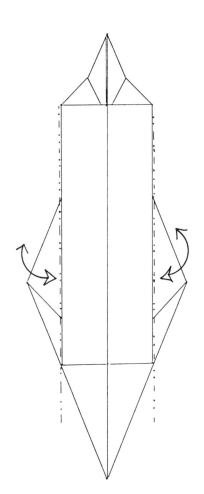

10. Crease along flap.

11.

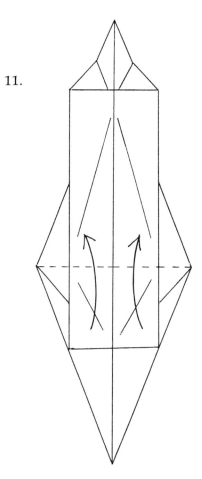

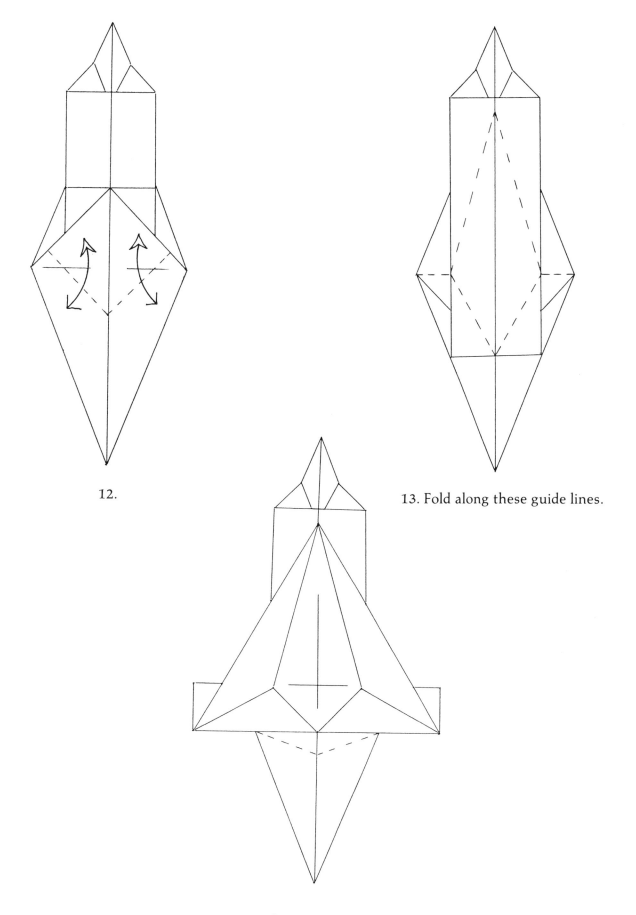

12.

13. Fold along these guide lines.

14.   Make Type *A* JET TAIL.

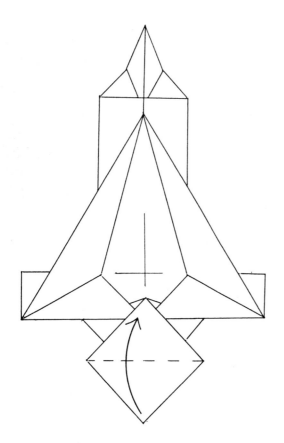

15. Turn over.

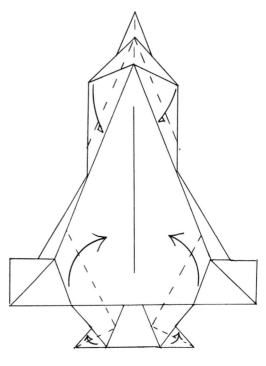

16.

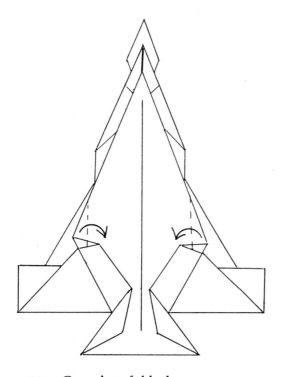

17. Complete fold, then turn over.

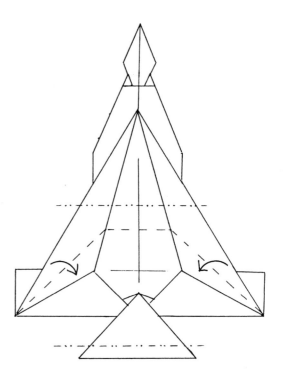

18. Look at step 19 for clarification.

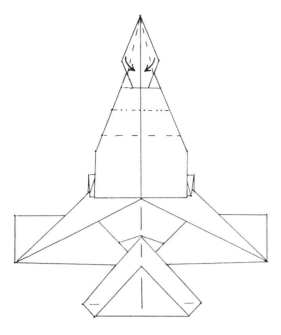

19.

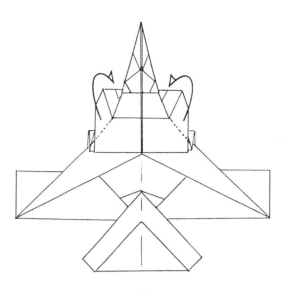

20.

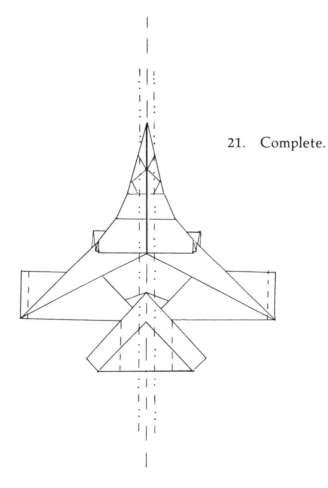

21.   Complete.

FIGHTER

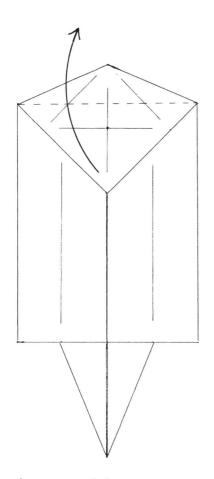

1. Begin with step 10 of the DOUBLE TAIL FIGHTER *except:* completely unfold the large flap and flatten it.

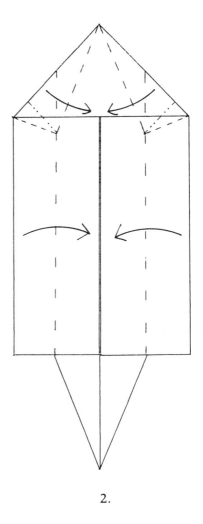

2.

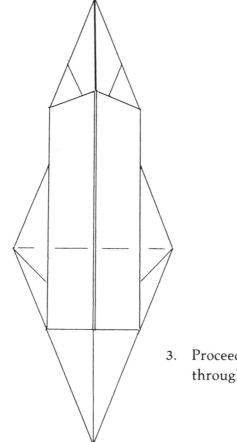

3. Proceed with DOUBLE TAIL FIGHTER steps 10 through 15 *except:* use Type *B* JET TAIL.

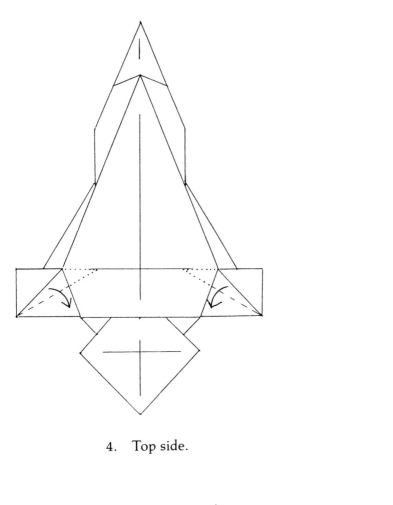

4. Top side.

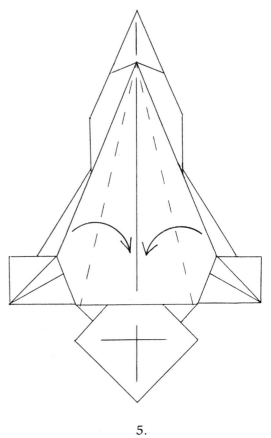

5.

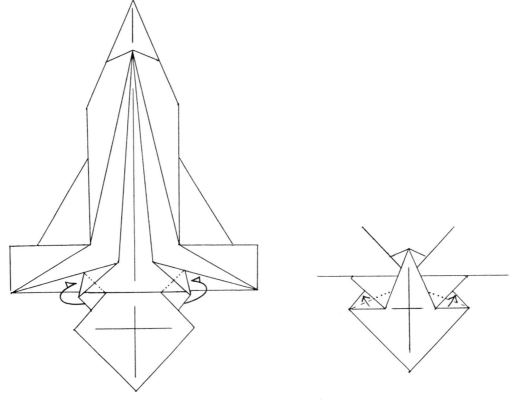

6. Top and bottom views of step.

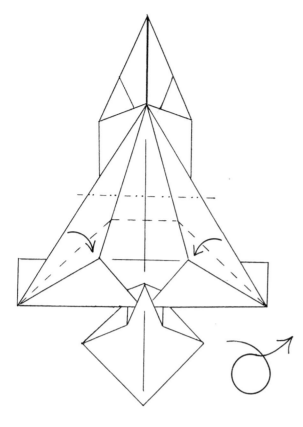

7.

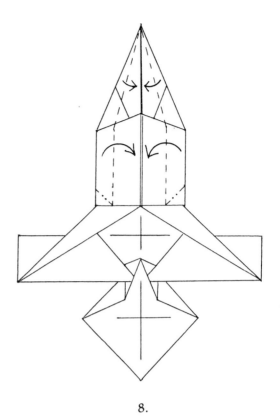

8.

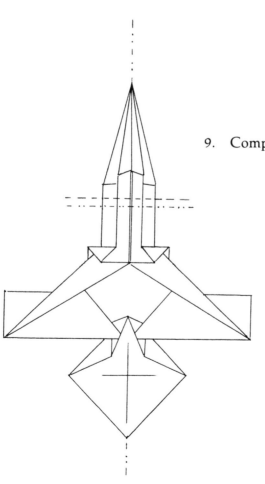

9.   Complete as necessary.

DART PLANE

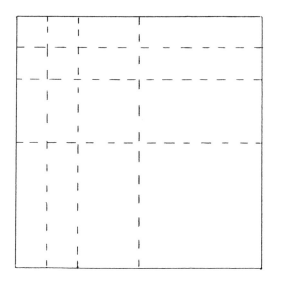

1. Make flaps.

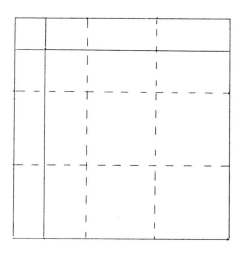

2. Fold into thirds.

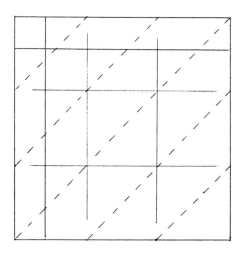

3.

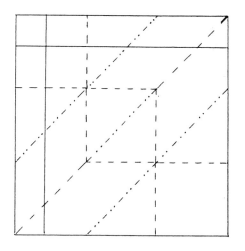

4. See step 5 for result.

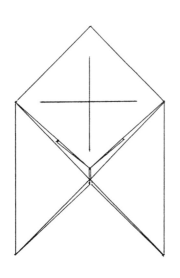

5.   Pull flap out.

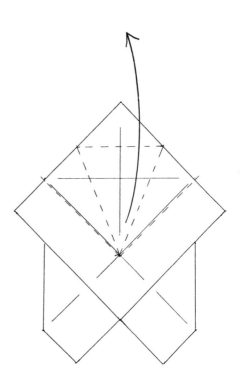

6.   Fold up as shown for this side . . .

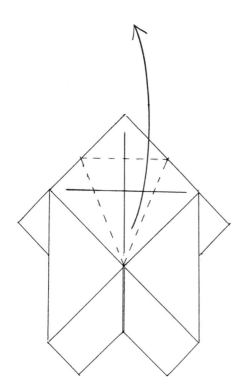

7.   . . . and the other side.

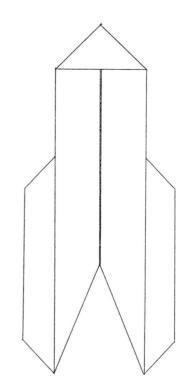

8.   Result of steps 5 and 6 with flap side up. Turn over.

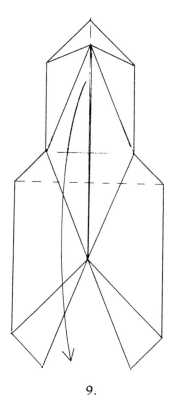

9.

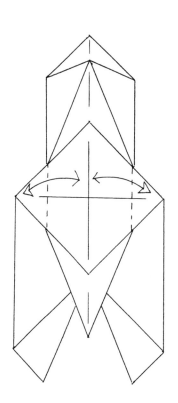

10.   Fold even with flap.

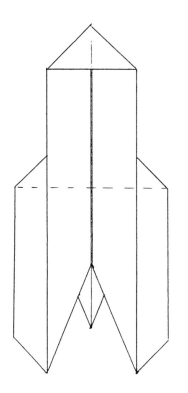

11.   Crease.

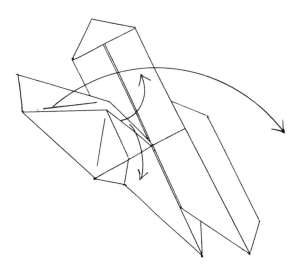

12.   Erect wing, separate layers, and flatten toward midline.

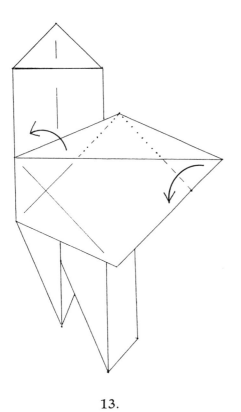

13.

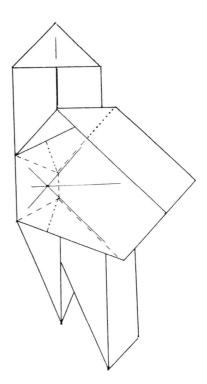

14. Look at step 15 for the proper completion of this fold.

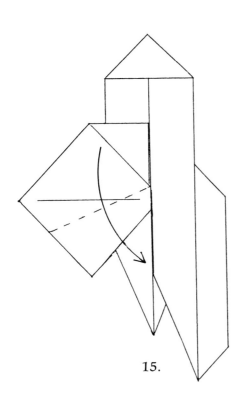

15.

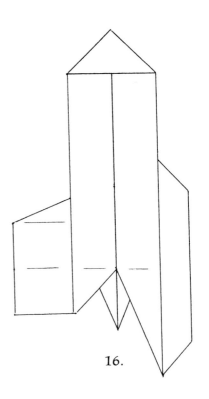

16.

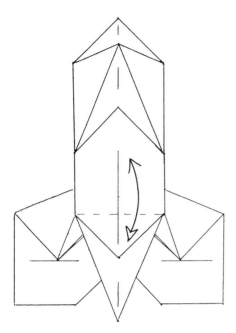

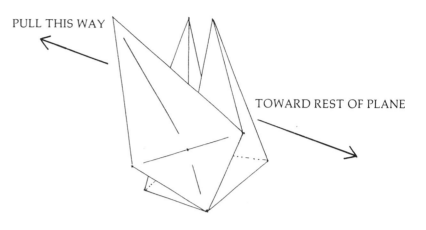

18. Note the mountain fold created when extending the model.

PULL THIS WAY

TOWARD REST OF PLANE

17. Crease as shown, then pull the point away from the rest of the body, extending its overall length.

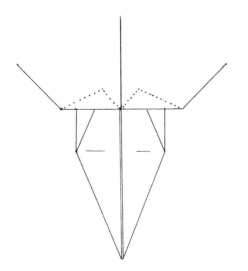

19. Completed extension.

20. Make the fold represented by the smallest arrow first.

Dart Plane   69

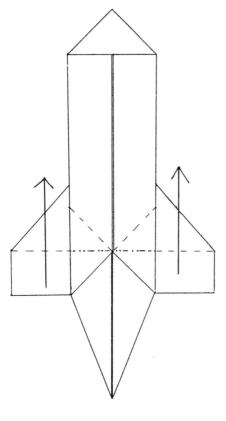

21.

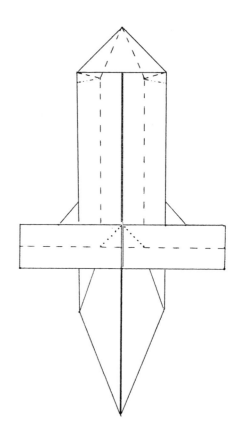

22. Make all folds concurrently. Look at step 23 for detail of wing/body junction.

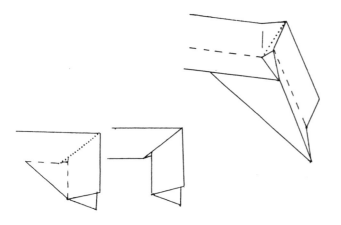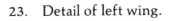

23. Detail of left wing.

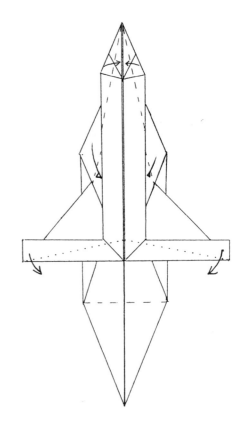

24. Expand wings.

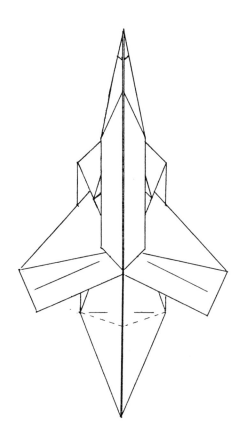

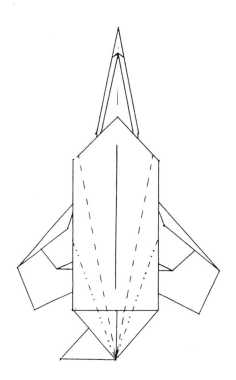

26. Make mountain fold first, then make valley fold through both layers.

25. Make JET TAIL to step 9. Turn over.

27.

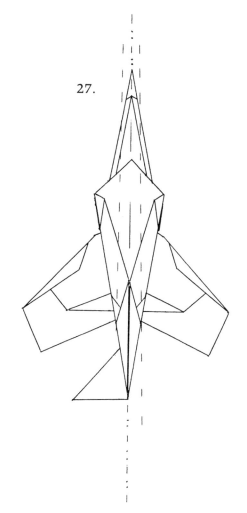

FIGHTER WITH ENGINES

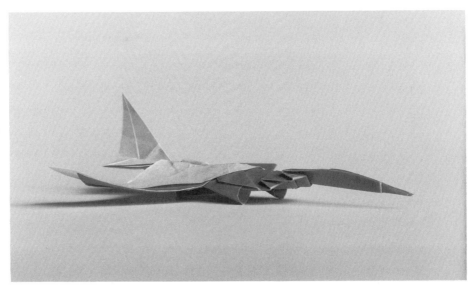

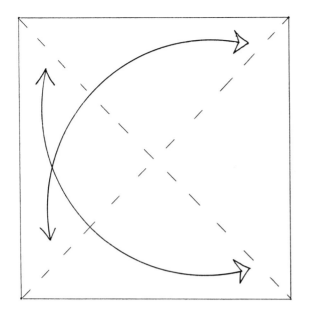

1.

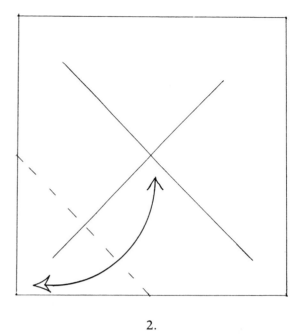

2.

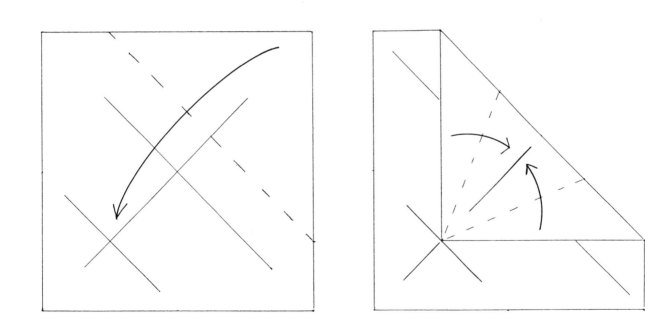

3.

4. Unfold model completely.

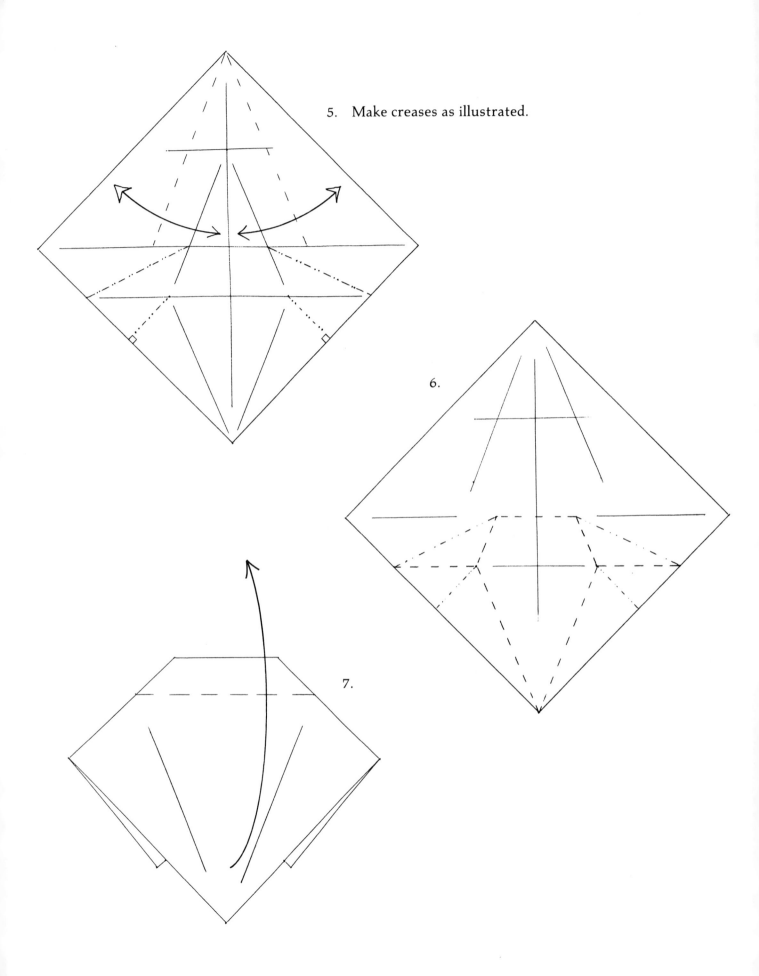

5. Make creases as illustrated.

6.

7.

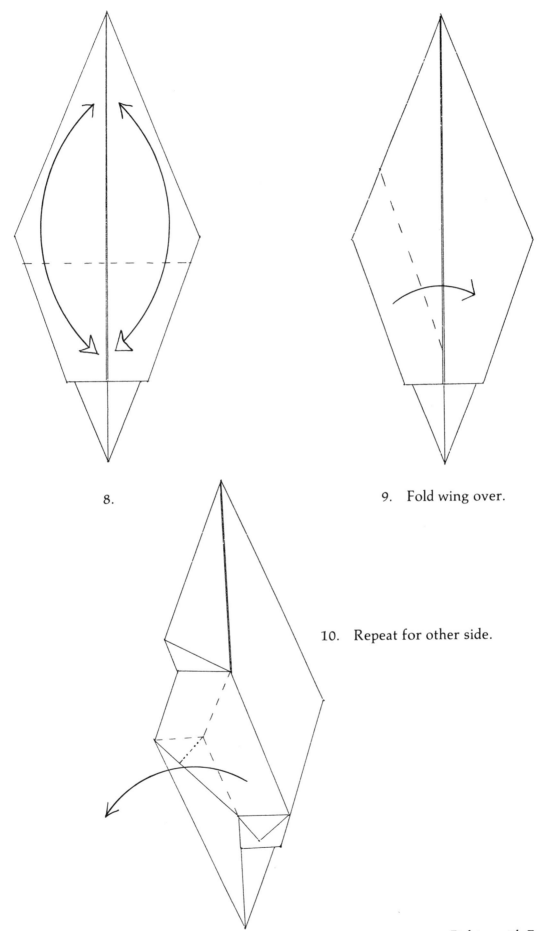

8.

9.   Fold wing over.

10.   Repeat for other side.

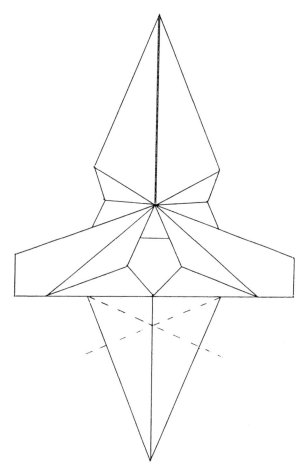

11.   Make JET TAIL . . .

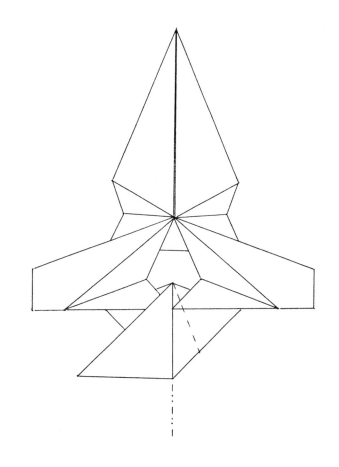

12.   . . . Type *A* . . .

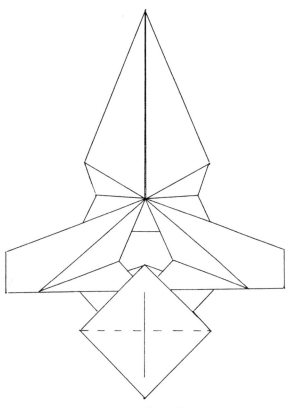

13.   . . . to get this. Turn over.

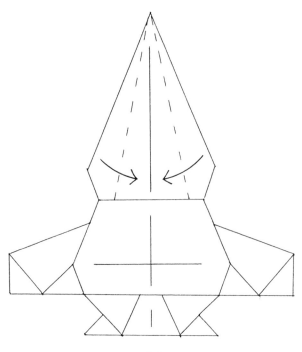

14.

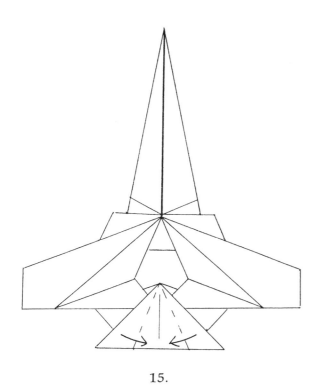

15.

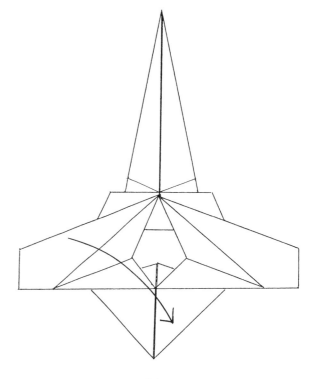

16.

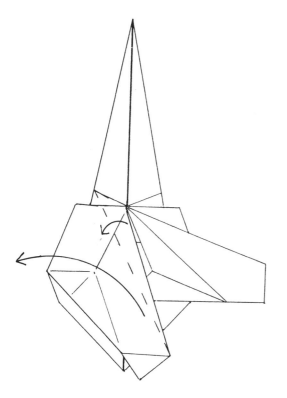

17. Fold small arrow first.

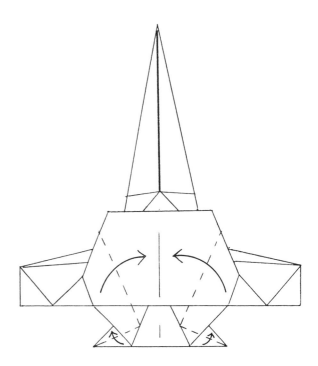

18. Make folds at same time.

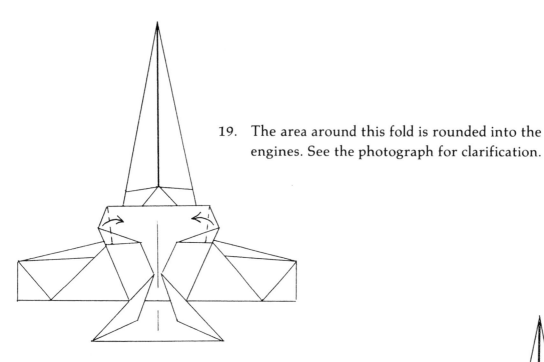

19. The area around this fold is rounded into the engines. See the photograph for clarification.

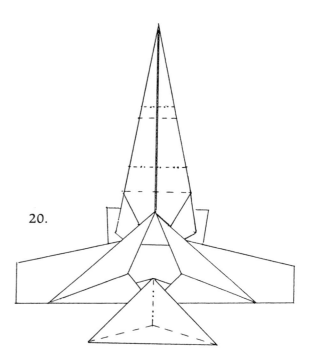

20.

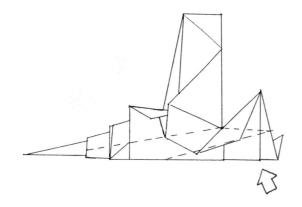

21. Push tail up by making a reverse fold. Round engines and form wings as with the INTERCEPTOR.

FUTURISTIC FIGHTER

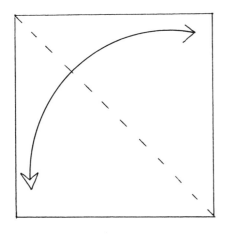

1.

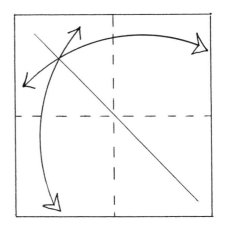

2.

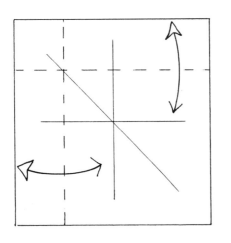

3.

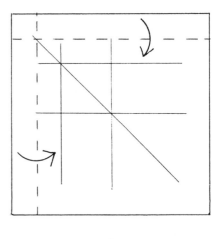

4.

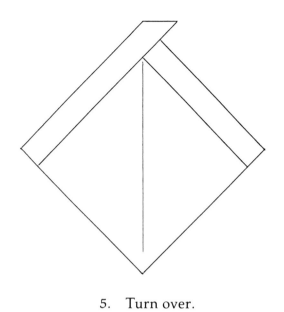

5.   Turn over.

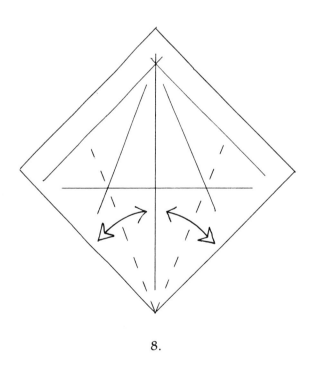

6.   Make fold then unfold model completely.

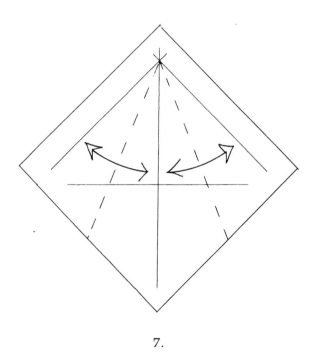

7.

8.

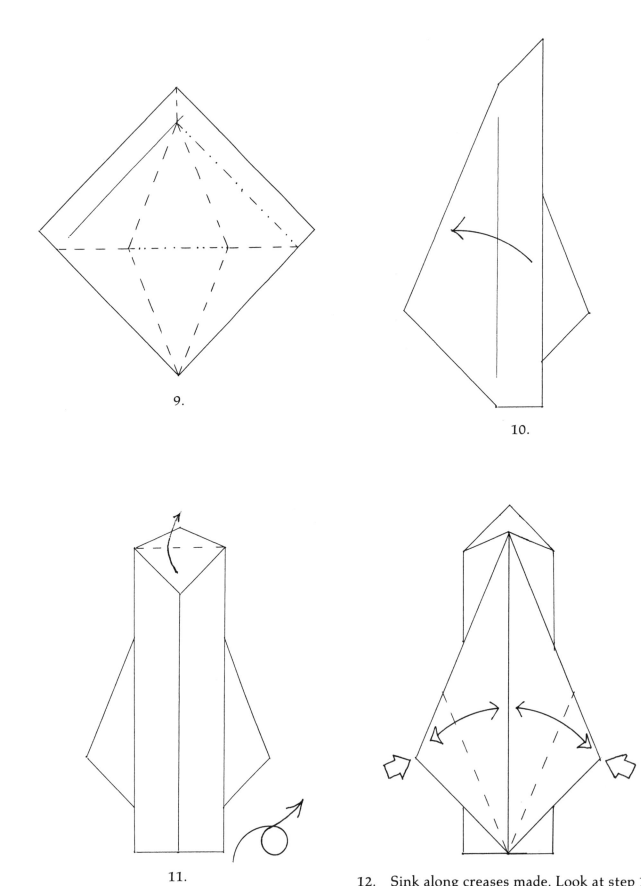

9.

10.

11.

12. Sink along creases made. Look at step 13.

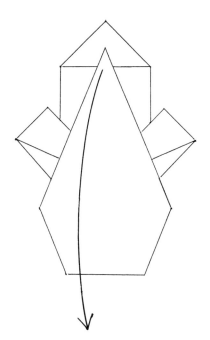

13. Result of step 12. Fold down while
    aligning wings parallel to axis of plane.

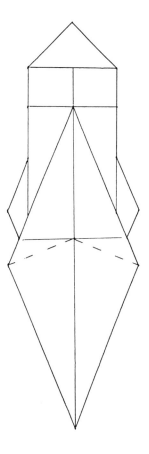

14. Erect wings, separate triangles, and flatten.
    The valley folds shown depict the angle at
    which the wings should be aligned.

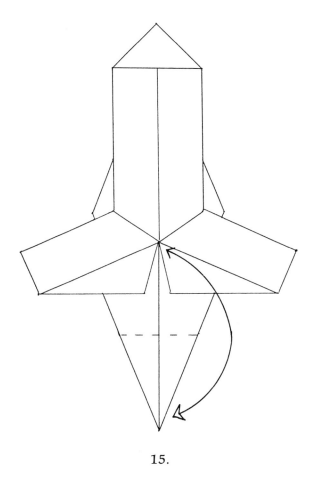

15.

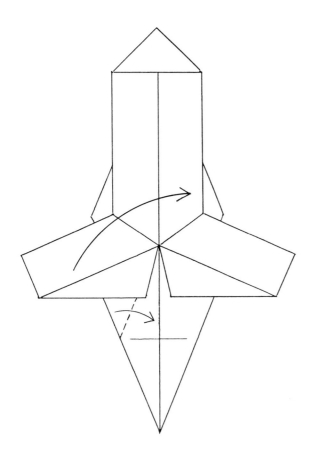

16. Fold wing over.

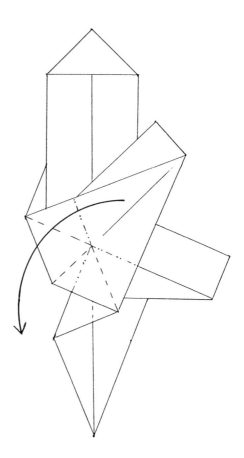

17. Fold wing back using folds shown.

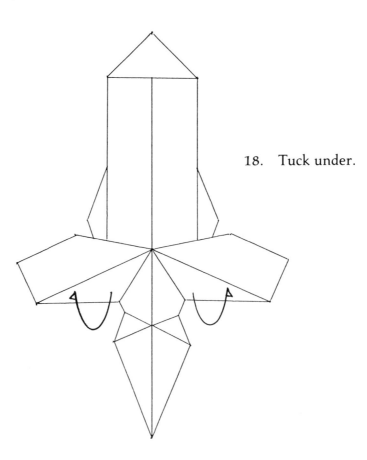

18. Tuck under.

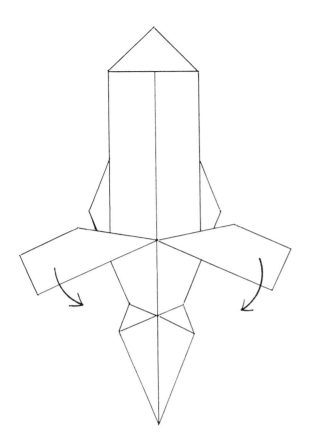

19.

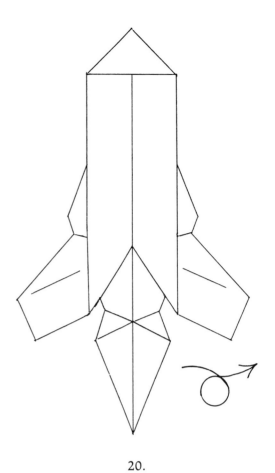

20.

21.

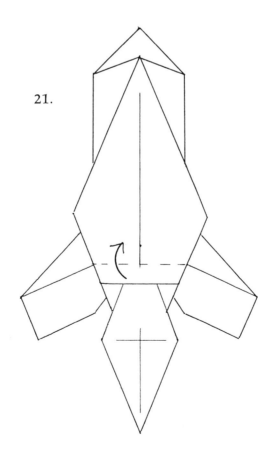

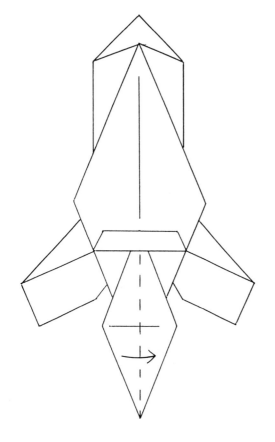

22.

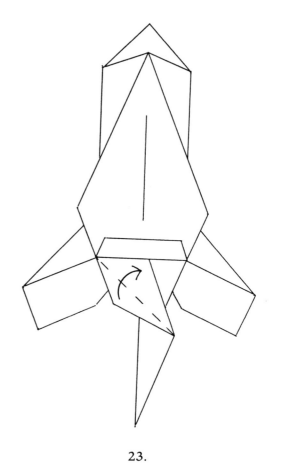

23.

24.

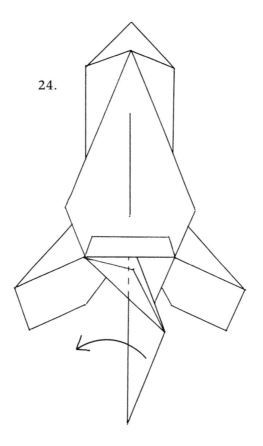

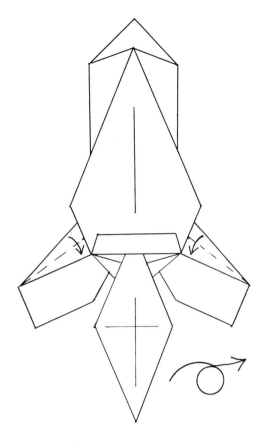

25.

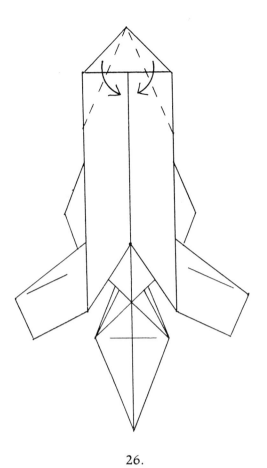

26.

27.

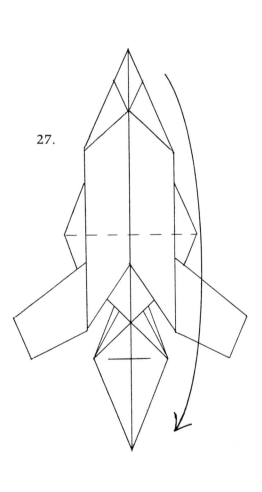

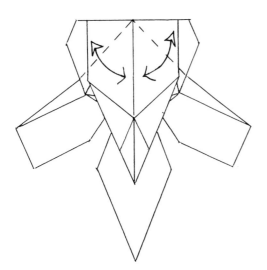

28. Unfold to step 27 after this step.

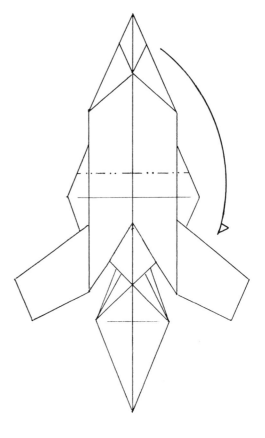

29.

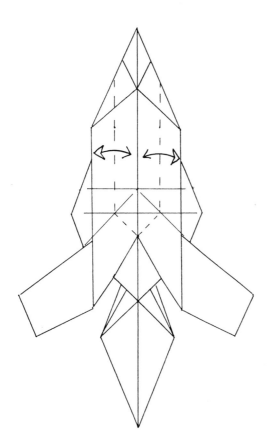

30. Prepare these creases.

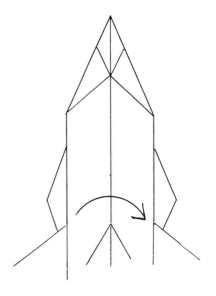

31.

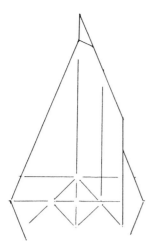

32.　All of these creases should exist.

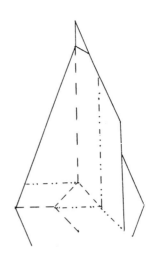

33.　Refold as shown. Repeat process for other side.

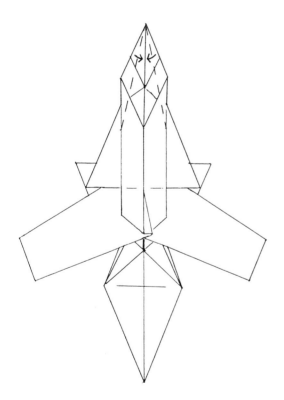

34.　Result of step 33.

35.

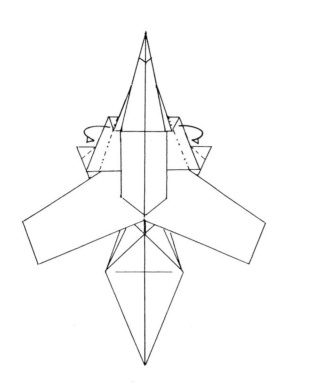

36. The valley folds make the wheels.

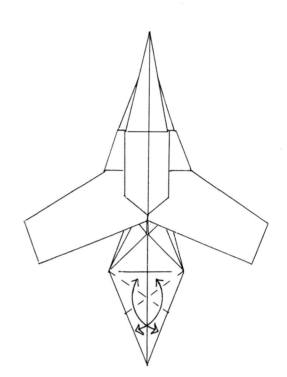

37. Make tail as shown.

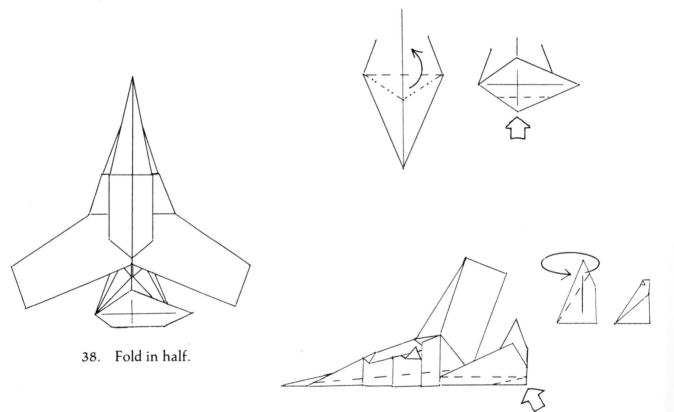

38. Fold in half.

39. Finish by making wings and refining the tail.

SOLUTIONS TO COMMON PROBLEMS

PROBLEM	PROBABLE CAUSES	SUGGESTED REPAIRS OR COUNTER-PROCEDURES
DIVES INTO GROUND	1) Wrong wing angle	refold wings or make up-flaps.
	2) Down-flaps too large	reduce flaps.
LOOPS	1) Too much lift	reduce airfoil or make down-flaps.
	2) Up-flaps too large	reduce flaps.
TURNS	1) Asymmetric axis	refold axis.
		make up-flap on same side as direction of turn.
		make down-flap on opposite side as direction of turn.
	2) Asymmetric flaps	reconsider function of flaps.
	3) Wing warping	flatten by refolding wings.
		make counter-flaps.
	4) Tail fin bent	straighten tail fin.
HOVERS/DOES NOT FLY	1) Bad weight distribution	make sure model is folded correctly.
	2) Too much air resistance	reduce cockpit and/or engine.
		reduce flap size if any.
		fold model more compactly.
VARIABLE FLIGHT	1) Plane thrown too hard	reduce thrust.
	2) Plane too flimsy	use thicker or smaller paper.
	3) Plane too rigid	use thinner or larger paper.
	4) Air space too windy	turn off air conditioner or heater.
PERSISTENT PROBLEMS	1) Improperly made	review procedure.
	2) Inaccurately folded	be more precise next time.